FOR ADDRESS
ONLY

19 01

MICH.

Miss Ethel Greve

22 Hamburg St

Muskegon

Mich

Dear Cindy + Pat,

We would never imagine you looking like the old couple leading off the "Marriage" section on "page 34" however we wish the "longivity" and happiness you both deserve.

Love,

Dan + Laurie
Fitzgerald

13 June, 1992

Have  Sand

Some

THE GRITTY SIDE OF LOVE

Have

Sand

Some

Suzanne Slesin, John Margolies, and Emily Gwathmey

Design by Adriane Stark

Clarkson Potter/Publishers·New York

THANK YOU TO **Roy Finamore,**
our editor, Bill Nave, and
Howard Klein at Clarkson
Potter; to **Adriane Stark,** our
designer; to **Lucy Kroll** and
Barbara Hogenson, our agents;
and to **Andreas Brown** at the
Gotham Book Mart.

"Unfortunate Coincidence" from *The*
Portable Dorothy Parker. Copyright
1926, 1954 by Dorothy Parker.
Reprinted by permission of Viking
Penguin, a division of Penguin Books,
USA Inc., and by permission of
Duckworth (Gerald Duckworth & Co Ltd).

Published by Clarkson Potter/Publishers,
201 East 50th Street, New York,
New York 10022. Member of the Crown
Publishing Group.

CLARKSON POTTER, POTTER, and colophon
are trademarks of Clarkson N. Potter, Inc.

Manufactured in Japan

Library of Congress Cataloging-in-
Publication Data
Have some sand : the gritty side of love
/ [compiled] by Suzanne Slesin, Emily
  Gwathmey, and John Margolies.
    1. Love—Humor.
2. Interpersonal relations—Humor.
I. Slesin, Suzanne.
II. Gwathmey, Emily.
III. Margolies, John. PN6231.L6H38
1992
306.7'0207—dc20   91–16573.
                                                    CIP

ISBN 0-517-58317-8

10 9 8 7 6 5 4 3 2 1

First Edition

other strangers

To lovers and

Contents

Ah love at the turn of the century. The little lady was evolving from a Gibson girl into a flapper. She was bobbing her hair, joining the work force, smoking in public, and experimenting with powder and rouge. Men were falling in love with the automobile. The telephone was still a newfangled invention, and communicating with a loved one was often left to the postcard.

Between 1900 and 1910, postcards quickly became a full-blown craze and reflected

We are looking for a man. —

every detail of the eternal battle of the sexes—from the playful seduction through the preordained rites of courtship, the inevitable marriages, and not-too-unexpected bouts of infidelity. **Ah, love** in the post-Victorian era. We think of this time fondly as one of innocence far removed from the cynical, sardonic point of view that we surely crafted in the sixties and seventies. But let's take a second look at those $5\frac{1}{2}$ X $3\frac{1}{2}$-inch missives that documented every flutter

of their correspon-
dents' hearts. Not
too far beneath the
surface of propri-
ety was a seething
sensuality that
Oscar Wilde and
Sigmund Freud
would comment
on—one pithily,
the other at great
length.
Very visible, in
fact, was a coy,
offbeat irrever-
ence, a naughty sense of
humor, a flip playfulness. In
our turbulent times, it's a sen-
sibility with which we are
quite in tune.
It's 1904. There they are together at the seashore. She's

wearing a long
skirt, a jacket, a
lace jabot, and a
smart hat. He's
all buttoned up
in a suit and tie.
She's smiling,
about to dump a
shovelful of sand
over him. A bit
unsure, he recoils
gracefully.
Nearly a hundred
years later, our
courting couple's
beach attire might be more
minimal, but the grains of
sand and the muddle of mixed
emotions are just as puzzling.
The tango continues. The more
things change the more they
remain the same.

CAN'T WE GET BETTER ACQUAINTED?

Seduction

Have some Sand

Every maiden's
weak
and willin'
When she
meets the
proper
villain.
—Clarence Day

A little woman is a dangerous thing. — Anonymous

WHEN ARE YOU COMING UP?

To fall in love you

have to be in the

state of mind for it

to take,

like a disease.

— Nancy Mitford

I like young girls. Their stories are shorter. —Thomas McGuane

Two Jacks, and Three Queens.

Can't we get better acquainted?

Tell me about yourself
—your struggles,
your dreams,
your telephone number.

—Peter Arno

Seduction

Anyone

for

tennis?

—Anony-

mous

IT'S ALL LOVE

698/

To be in love is merely to be in a state

Bending low, her hand he takes
And presses it softly as she wakes.

A netting for kissing bugs

of perpetual anesthesia. — H. L. Mencken

He gave her a look
you could have
poured on a waffle.

—Ring Lardner

Seduction

Now, be good, M.. Good.

Have a Chair, Mr. Good.

Most women set out to try to change a man, and when they have changed him, they do not like him.
—Marlene Dietrich

No.6

Oh; how good.

THE MICROBE FACTORY

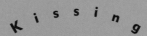

Kissing

BE PLAIN IN dress,
and sober in
your diet;
In short, my
deary, kiss
me, and be quiet.
—Lady Mary
Wortley Montagu

Kiss till the cows come home.—Beaumont and Fletcher

A Gable Spoon.

"Stop your fooling, Charlie"

A kiss:

The

anatomical

juxtaposition

of two

orbicularis

oris muscles

in a

state of

contraction.

—Dr. Henry

Gibbons

A Microbe Factory.

You have to kiss an awful lot of frogs

before you find a prince. — BBC Radio 4

A kiss can be a comma,
a question mark, or an
exclamation point.
That's basic spelling
that every woman ought
to know.
—Mistinguette

A LISPING lass
is good
to kiss.
— John Ray

TULIPS

Love me, love my umbrella. —James Joyce

Betrothal

A fool and his money are soon married. —Carolyn Wells

One should always

be wary of anyone who

promises that their

love will last longer

than a weekend.

—Quentin Crisp

If you've got the money
stay right here.

The trouble
        with some
women is
        that they
get all
        excited
about nothing
        —and then
marry him.
        —Cher

A peach of a mash and
    A bunch of cash   Can you beat it?

Love is what happens to men and women who don't

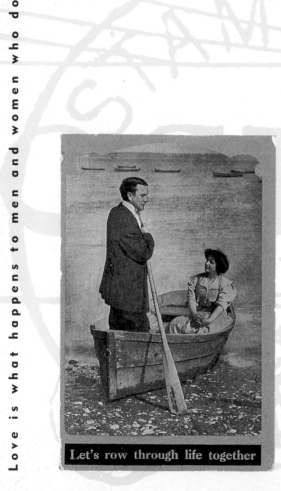

Let's row through life together

BY THE TIME you
swear you're his
Shivering and sighing,
And he vows his pas·sion is
Infinite, undying—
Lady, make a note of this:
One of you is lying.
—Dorothy Parker

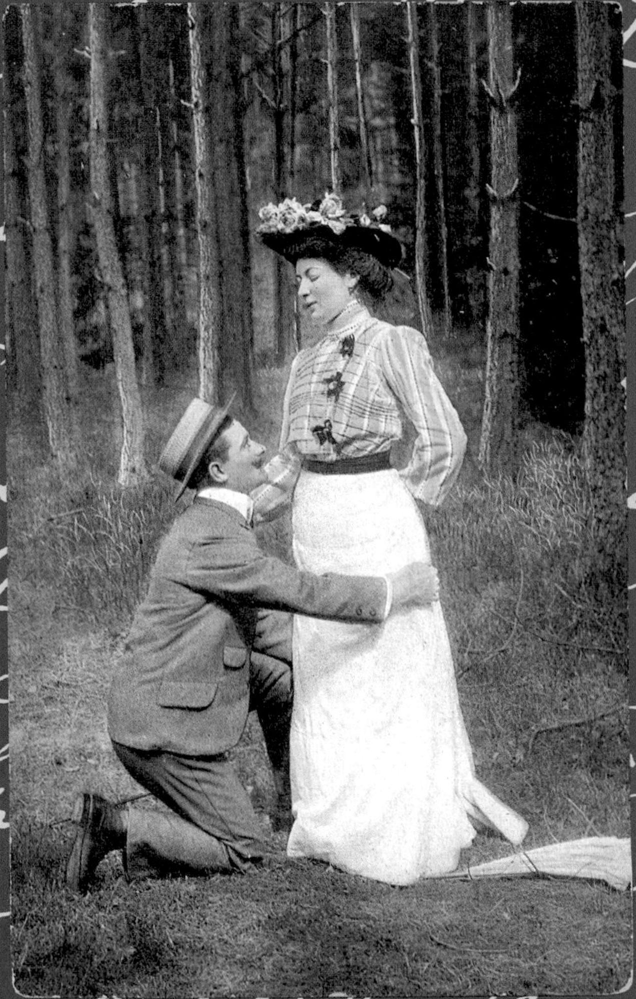

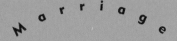

Marriage

MARRYING A MAN is like buying something you've been admiring for a long time in a shop window. You may love it when you get it home, but it doesn't always go with everything else in the house.
—Jean Kerr

Get married, but never to a man who is home all day. —George Bernard Shaw

Don't worry it'll all come out in the wash.—

The most happy marriage I can picture ... would be the union of a deaf man to a blind woman. —Samuel Taylor Coleridge

He loves me — He loves me not.—

Marriage

Forty years
    of romance
make a
    woman look
like a ruin
    and forty
years of
    marriage
make her
    look like
a public
    building.
—Oscar Wilde

Ah, Mozart! He was happily married —but his wife wasn't.
—Victor Borge

Marriage is a wonderful invention;

but then again so is a bicycle repair kit. — Billy Connolly

The concept of two people living together for twenty-five years without having a cross word suggests a lack of spirit only to be admired in sheep. — A. P. Herbert

Never go

to bed mad.

Stay up

and fight.

—Phyllis Diller

A STRIKING BEAUTY. –

I LOVE MY WIFE, BUT OH YOU GUMDROP!

Infidelity

THE OFT'NER seen,
the more I lust,
The more I lust,
the more I smart,
The more I smart,
the more I trust,
The more I trust,
the heavier heart,
The heavy heart
breeds mine unrest,
Thy absence therefore
I like best.
—Barnaby Goodge

AM WELL TAKEN CARE OF HERE-- BUT TOO BUSY TO WRITE

You don't seem to realise that in married life

I AM WORKING HARD.
IN HARTFORD, CONN.

THINGS SEEM PRETTY TIGHT HERE.

three is company, and two is none.—Oscar Wilde

Infidelity

But I wasn't
kissing her.
I was whispering
in her mouth.

—Chico Marx

For a while we pondered

whether to take a

vacation or get a

divorce. We decided that

My wife won't let me -

a trip to Bermuda is over

in two weeks, but a

divorce is something you

always have.

—Woody Allen

Alice, where art thou?

PHOTO ONLY COPYRIGHT 1908
BY BAMFORTH & CO

Say! but that Card
is O.K. No you do
not look loneson
Oh! what do I kn
about you! I han
been hearing som
good news. I am